CW01604206

Contents

In the name of Allah (SWT), Most Gracious, Most Merciful

May Allah accept this work through His Grace and grant all Muslims with knowledge, courage and steadfastness. Aameen.

This workbook about Ramadan is for you. You can read and write about your Ramadan.

There are signs in the workbook which tells you what to do:

 Studying and reciting Quran or hadith.

 An activity to do

 Writing, making notes

 Reading and thinking

 Key for solutions

 Time management

 your parents/carers/teachers to see
And sign your work.

Allah (SWT) will give you lots of rewards for your efforts to know more about your deen. May Allah (SWT) bless you and your family and make it easy for you all to learn.

About the Moon

The sun, moon and stars

How wonderful is the sight of the sun, the moon and the stars. It is the Control of Allah (SWT) to let the sun rise and warm the earth.
Allah (SWT) makes the stars shine at their fixed place and let the moon shine as a gentle light in the dark night.Studying science explains the purpose of what Allah (SWT)has created in His Wisdom. In the Quran you read in chapter 6, Al-An-Aam.

Praise be to Allah(SWT),
Who created the Heavens
And the Earth.
And made the Darkness
And the Light. 6;1

The moon calendar

To calculate the time, the Islamic calendar is following the moon. The changes in the shapes of the moon are the phases of the moon. A moon month has 29 or 30 days. It starts with the sight of the new moon. The moon will grow day by day bigger. This is called waxing. When the moon is shrinking and getting smaller this is called waning. When the new moon is seen again the month has ended, the new month has started.

You can follow the moon from the beginning of Ramadan till the end by colouring the circles as you see the moon every night.

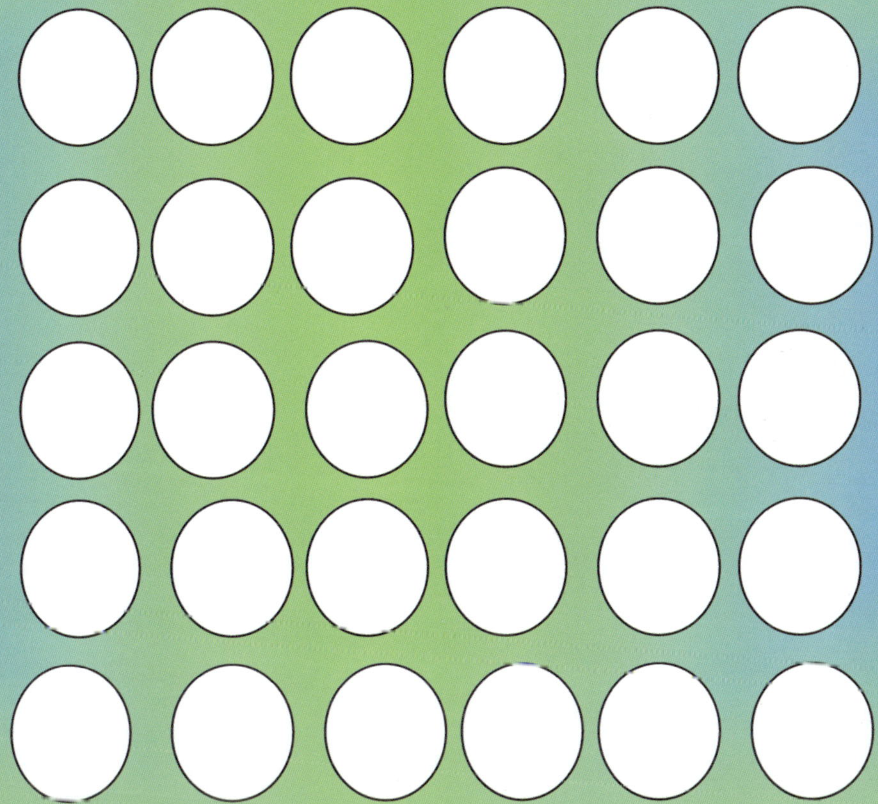

It's almost Ramadan

Your house

Your house is the place where you spend time with your family. It is the place where you are comfortable. The house is a place that needs to be tidy.

- In a tidy house you can easily find the things you need; you won't lose time with searching.
- Also your values are kept safe.
- In the house you offer your prayers and read Quran.

Can you think of more reasons?

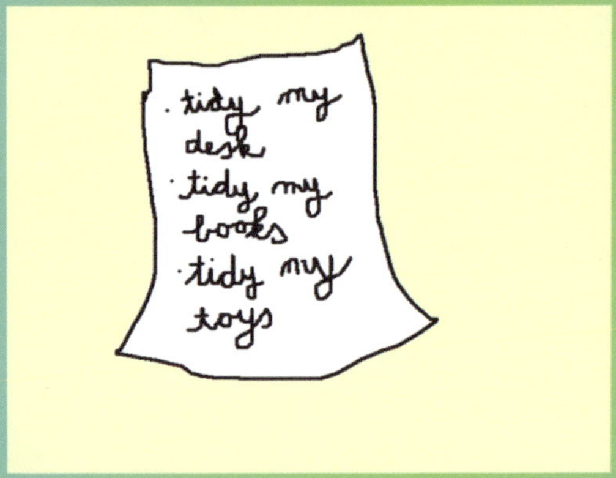

Are there any things you don't need to keep? Discuss this with your parents and give away what you don't need to the right person or organisation. *Keep your house a nice place to live.*

Say Bismillah before you start anything

Everyone in the house can help to keep the house tidy and organised. Little children can help with small tasks. Older children can do more difficult jobs. Which job can you do? Here are some ideas to get you started:

Throwing the bin bags in the bin-watering the plants-washing the car-shoe polishing-cutting vegetables-organising the book shelves-taking laundry from the dryer or the line.......

Can you make a list for every one`s jobs?

It will help to create time for the whole family to read Quran and doing other good deeds.

Verily Allah knows all the hidden things
Of the heavens and the earth:
Verily He has full knowledge of all that is
In men's hearts. 35-38

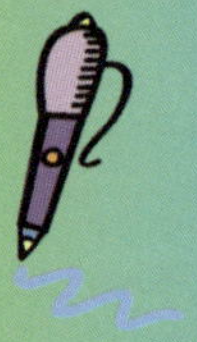

Talk regularly about aya's from the Holy Quran and discuss what it means.

Time the minutes of this activity and keep a record of it. It gives you an idea how much time we really put in activities like this.

Starting time of the activity	The activity description	The ending time	What did you achieve

Ramadan Mubarak

In Ramadan you don't want to lose time with doing a lot of shopping. It's precious time that you want to spend on good deeds, reading Quran and doing extra prayers.

We can make shopping lists and do most of the shopping in advance. You can help with making a good shoppinglist and help with the shopping. In Ramadan Muslims have their special dishes so make sure you have the right ingredients. What are you cooking in Ramadan? Add later the prices of the shopping and the money you spend. It is good to learn the prices to know how you spend money. You know why?

article	Amount	Price

Help your parents wherever you can
Also if they don't ask

Cooking

Helping your mum or dad with cooking is very nice, especially a meal where everyone is waiting for like the iftar!

Draw here the recipe what you would like to cook.

Where did you find this recipe?

The name of the recipe is

The ingredients are:

This is the way to do it.

How much time did it take?

Think about this...and tell what it means...

Abu Huraira (RA) narrates that Allah's Messenger (SAW) said:" The food of two people is sufficient for three, and the food of three persons is sufficient for four."

The first day of Ramadan

Try to fast days of Ramadan, but make sure you eat and drink before dawn. After that the day of fasting starts and we cannot eat and drink anymore till sunset. Put your alarm in the right time and wake up the others if they are still asleep... The breakfast before dawn is called suhoor and there are blessings in the suhoor.

- It is the sunnah
- It gives strength for ibadah
- It helps not to become angry. What happens sometimes because of feeling hungry ?

Don't forget your alarm!

Ibn Umar (RA) relates: Rasullulah(SAW) said: "Verily ALLAH (SWT) and His Malaaikah send Mercy upon those who eat Suhoor."

What is your favourite breakfast?

Can you help to prepare the breakfast? Ask your family the day before what they like and try to make it with your mum or dad. Fruit salad is a tasty starter of the day and most people love it.

Give everyone a hadith of the day written on a little paper. And at the Iftar you can ask if they did something with the lesson.

Sweets

No sweets the whole day can be a challenge as well...Which sweets or dessert you like most? At the end of the fasting day it is a special treat for you.

Well done, not eating and drinking a whole day is a sign of strength.

For the little ones you can make a **paper chain** with sweets. At the end of the day, they can have their sweets of the day. During the day they don't eat sweets. In this way they can have the feeling of what fasting is as well.

Narrated by Abu Huraira(RA) :" The Prophet (SAW) never criticized any food (he was invited to), but he used to eat if he liked the food, and left it if he disliked it."

Share your ideas and discuss how to organise them. Write them down and stick them on an organiser board so everyone can read it as well in his own time.

Salah

Once the prophetMuhammad (SAW)came out of his house and it was autumn and the leaves were falling off the trees. He caught hold of a branch of a tree and its leaves began to drop in a large number. At this he remarked, O, Abuzar! (RA) when a Muslim offers his salah to please Allah, his sins are shed away from him just as these leaves are falling off this tree. "(narrated by AbuzarRA)

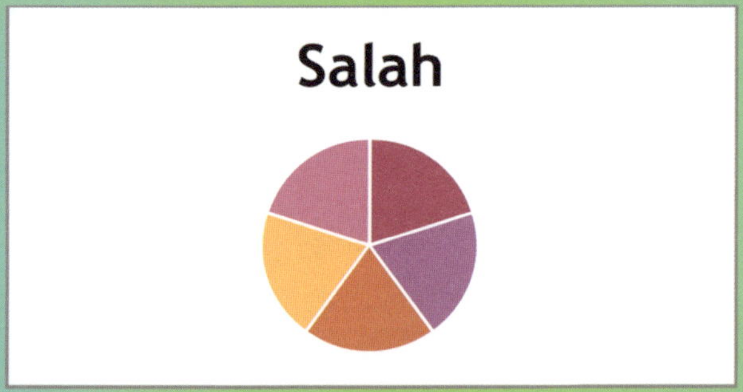

Mark your prayers chart

Day	Fajr	Zohr	Asr	Magrib	Isha
Monday					
Tuesday					
Wednesday					
Thursday					
Friday					
Saturday					
Sunday					

Abu Hurairah(RA) narrates that once Rasullullah(SAW) asked his companions, Do you believe that dirt can remain on a person bathing five times a day in a brook running in front of his door?' No, replied the companions, No dirt can stay on his body.' Rasullullah(SAW) remarked:' So, exactly similar is the effect of salah offered five times a day. With the Grace of Allah (SWT), it washes away all the sins.'

Day	Fajr	Zohr	Asr	Magrib	Isha
Monday					
Tuesday					
Wednesday					
Thursday					
Friday					
Saturday					
Sunday					

Day	Fajr	Zohr	Asr	Magrib	Isha
Monday					
Tuesday					
Wednesday					
Thursday					
Friday					
Saturday					
Sunday					

Iftar

After prayer the second obligatory duty for a Muslim is to fast in the month of Ramadan. It is such a good training and we will benefit from it so much Insha Allah. What we do in Ramadan?

We don't eat and drink from dawn till sunset. Through fasting you learn to control yourself at difficult moments. You also learn to do your things in moderation. That means not too much from everything. That is the best way to keep everything healthy and strong.
But Allah (SWT) does not make the exercise too difficult for us. We can eat and drink again at sunset. That is a Mercy form Allah (SWT) to make it possible for us to achieve. And Allah (SWT) knows us best.

To encourage yourself in the day you fast, you can colour your progress of fasting every day in this chart. This is how it works. You colour a square when an hour of fasting has passed. At last you can fill in the time of iftar.

Day starting time finishing time

day																		

Motivate yourself to keep fasting with, you can do it! Write motivating words on a note and stick it on a place where everyone walks regularly. It will help others as well to feel strong.

Rasullulah (SWT) has said:

"If my Ummah would realise what Ramadan really is, they would wish that the whole year round should be Ramadan."

Day1	Start																	
Day2																		
Day3																		
Day4																		
Day5																		
Day6																		
Day7																		
Day8																		
Day9																		
Day10																		
Day11																		
Day12																		
Day13																		
Day14																		
Day15																		
Day16																		

Day17																		
Day18																		
Day19																		
Day20																		
Day21																		
Day22																		
Day23																		
Day24																		
Day25																		
Day26																		
Day27																		
Day28																		
Day29																		
Day30																		

O You who believe! Fasting is prescribed for you as it was prescribed for those before you, that you may become Al Muttaqun(the pious)2:183

Honouring guests

Welcoming guests in your house is a joyous occasion and a chance for rewards. The sunnah of the Prophet Muhammad (SAW)was that he made his guests feel most welcome and he was most generous.

- Welcome your guests warmly with salaam and a smile
- Sit with your guests and show happiness that they are visiting you
- Give them extra attention; ask about them.
- Especially to foreigners who have no family and friends around
- Give generously what you can give
- Switch off television

Make your own invitations for guests

It would be nice to invite your friends at home to have an iftar with you. Honouring your guests gives you awards from Allah (SWT). You can send them a self made invitation.

This is just an example of an invitation. I am sure you have much better ideas!

Work precisely, so your Your invitation looks good.

Mint tea

After the dinner you can surprise your friends with a nice cup of tea. Mint is a healthy plant and it gives a fresh and lovely taste to the tea.

Boil water in a teapot or pan with green tea leaves. Then you add the mint leaves and let it boil together. Add sugar according to taste and serve it in little tea glasses.

If you are invited, bring something for your friends like cookies or a nice juice.

'Whoever believes in Allah and the last day let him be generous to his guest in what he gives.'
Bukhari(RA)

Du'aa

The inside of a nut is what is really liked for eating. Du'aa is like the inside of the nut. It is the most important form of worshipping Allah (SWT). Why?

Allah loves it that we ask Him and that we understand that everything comes from Him. When you make du'aa you accept The Greatness of Allah (SWT).

Make sure at the time you make Du'aa:

- Be in wudu
- Face the qiblah
- Do good deeds before you make du'aa
- Raise your hands with a small gap between the hands
- First praise Allah (SWT)
- Concentrate on Allah (SWT)
- Feel small when you ask
- Repeat the du'aa
- Don't look at the sky
- End with Ameen and wipe your hands over your face
- and believe Allah(SWT)will accept your du'aa

Try to find a du'aa in the Quran or Hadith

Enjoy doing research

At the time of iftar we are mostly so focused on eating that we forget to make du'aa. Remember! The du'aa of the fasting person is accepted.

Try to learn the sedu'aas from the Quran by heart.

"O Allah (SWT) for You have I fasted, in You do I believe, and on You do I rely, and now I break this fast with food coming from You."

"O Allah (SWT), I beg You, through Your infinite Mercy, which surrounds all things, to forgive me."

Write a du'aa in your own words start with praising Allah(SWT).

Organise your study time And make a list with goals to focus on.

We go to the mosque

In Ramadan we pray extra special prayers after salatul isha. These are the *tarawih* prayers. Try to go every night and colour each time.

Ramadan is the time to increase your acts of worship! Divide Ramadan in three periods of 10 days.

When you attended the mosque, colour your chart, start in the first row top down.

Ramadan	Ramadan	Ramadan
Ramadan	Ramadan	Ramadan
Ramadan	Ramadan	Ramadan
Ramadan	Ramadan	Ramadan
Ramadan	Ramadan	Ramadan
Ramadan	Ramadan	Ramadan
Ramadan	Ramadan	Ramadan
Ramadan	Ramadan	Ramadan
Ramadan	Ramadan	Ramadan
Ramadan	Ramadan	Ramadan

Respect the mosque with two rakat prayer when you arrive.

Good deeds

You know how it feels when someone is helpful to you or speaks nicely to you when you struggle with a task.

Some acts seem small but they can really make a difference. When you walk to school and you remove a banana skin from the pavement is a good thing. You can avoid that someone can make a bad fall. It helps to think what you won't like and to avoid that others won't feel in that way.

With the table you can make notes of your good deeds

Especially in Ramadan good deeds will be **70** times more rewarded.

Nice to your parents							
Smiling is sadaqah							
Helping others							

Identify the chance to do a good deed. Every little helps!

Keep calm when getting angry							
Reading Quran Performing obligatory prayers							
Visiting the elderly and sick							
Performing non-obligatory prayers							
Zikr Tasbih Tahlil Takbir							

The night of power

One of the last ten nights of Ramadan is the night in which the Quran was revealed for the first time. This night is called *LailatulQadr*. It is better than a thousand months. The Quran is the most important book for Muslims. The angel *Gibraeel* came in this night to teach the first words to the prophet Muhammad (SAW).

If a Muslim is praying in this night and asking Allah (SWT) for something, Allah (SWT) will give it to him.

Search LailatulQadr in the last ten days of Ramadan. These nights the Muslims perform extra prayers. Some people follow the example of the prophet Muhammad (SAW)to stay for ten days in the masjid. This is called I'tikaf.You can bring food/drinks to the Muslims in I'tikaf.

Find the surah about LailatulQadr in the Quran and copy it here.

Ask help if needed and remember making mistakes is natural; you learn from mistakes.

Shadowplay

One day you can treat your family or friends with a shadow story. It works like this. First you think of a short story with a lesson in it. Cut the shapes form cardboard and stick them on sticks. You can try to make them move and play with them. Hang a white sheet. Place a table behind it with a lamp on it and let it shine on the sheet. Play the shapes behind the sheet and before the lamp. While all the other lights are switched off. Write the text in here of your best story so far!

Allahumma Innaka Afuwwan Tuhibbul Afwa Fa Fu Annee
O Allah (SWT) You are the Best Forgiver, the Beneficient and Merciful. You love forgiveness so forgive me. Can you say and write it in Arabic?

Make sure your play is attractive by using different voices and don't speak too soft or quick.

The Quran

The Quran is the Word of Allah (SWT). To read the Quran we need to be extra careful.The sunnah teaches us how to performs deeds of ibadah, worship. Before you start reading the Quran remember these sunnats.

- Be clean by wudu,
- Sit in a quiet place facing the Kaaba, that means towards Makah,
- Sit in a respectful way

If you want to get extra rewards organise with your friends to set up a help project. For example: cleaning the masjid. Cleanliness is very important. Especially the places of prayer!

Remember good deeds done regularly are rewarded more!!!Make sure that you have

- a timetable with the dates of cleaning
- a description of the tasks
- more children who can help regularly
- some of the parents who can supervise

Make gentle reminders by writing posters and ask the Muslims who come and pray to keep the masjid clean and tidy.

Prepare yourself before you start an activity. ***Remember the sunnah rules.***

Reciting the Quran

Recite the Quran in a correct way:

- Slowly
- In a low voice
- In a melodious voice
- Imagine you are reciting to Allah (SWT)
- Pause and think about the meaning of the words
- Keep thinking you are reading the sublime words of Almighty Allah
- Love reading Quran

Record the first time you read a surah. Start practising and remind yourself with the above points.

After a week you recite again and record it as well. Now listen to the first time and then to the recitation after a week of practising. You hear the difference?

Enjoy your progress! Every step forward is a step closer to your success. Make a timeline, so you can see your progress.
Fill a jar with marbles, coins or something else with every step of progress.

The Quran is a source

Imagine the place where the river starts flowing...it gives and gives and makes its way through the landscape. The river gives life to plants and all kind of water animals live in there. The people use the river for fishing and crossing the river to visit each other.
The start of the river is a source.
The Holy Quran is also a source. It is a source of advice. Allah speaks to us through the Quran and gives us advice about how to deal with all kind of matters in life. And when you live according to these advices you will see that good things come from it. Find in the Quran and fill in three advices.

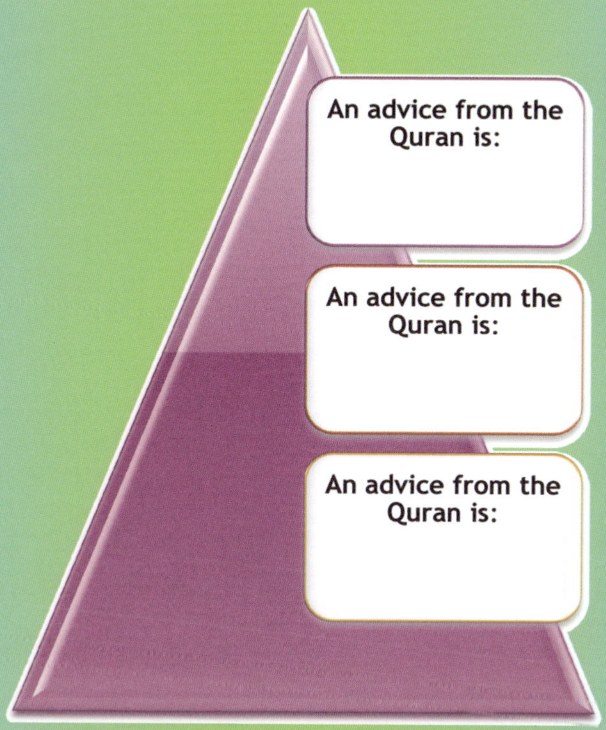

Treat the Quran with respect

Reading in Arabic

...And Allah (SWT) is The Protector of those who have faith. (3-68)

The Quran is written in Arabic. Any Quran in another language is a translation.

If you learn to read the Quran in Arabic, it is exactly the way Allah (SWT) revealed it to the prophet Muhammad (SAW).

We pray in Arabic. Therefore do your best to learn to read and write in Arabic and you will be able to fully understand the Words of Allah (SWT).

Understanding these words is the best thing in life and will give you so much joy and happiness.

Study Quran

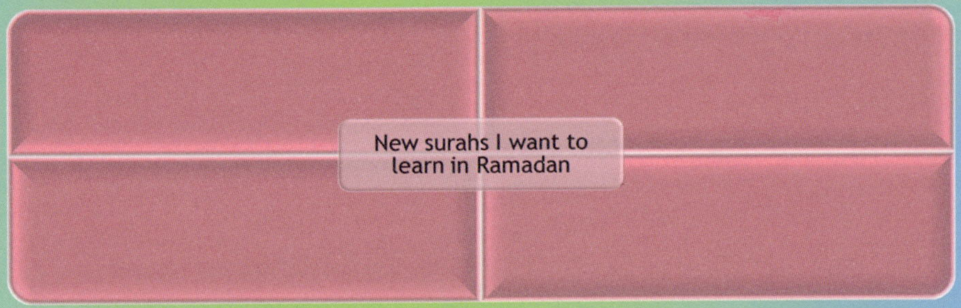

Make a time planning for learning a new and schedule how to learn a new surah. Write down the steps and practice daily

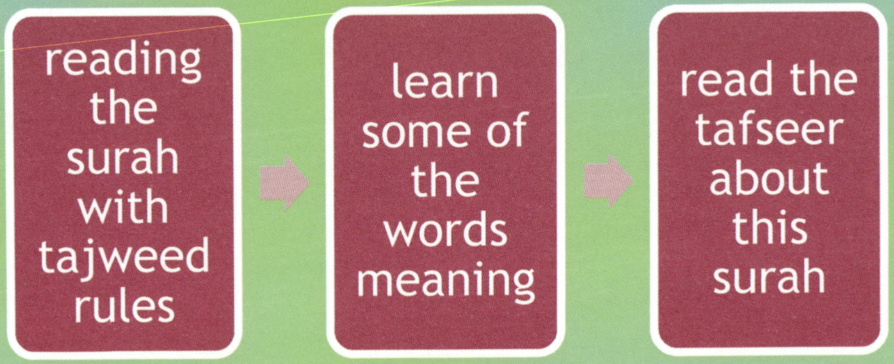

Zakat

People need money to buy their food, clothes and transport. It is very important that the money you use is coming from halal sources. This means that you earned the money in a way Allah is pleased with. Important questions are:

- Where is this money from?
- How did I get this money?

Not all the money we should keep for ourselves. It is important to keep some money for charity. You give money to people who need it. It is *sadaqah*.

Zakat

Zakat is the money you have to give. For this is a calculation. Allah (SWT) gave us the information how much we should pay from our valuables that we own. For example you have 5000 in the bank and you didn't need to use this money for living. 2.5% of this amount of money you need to give as zakat that year.

Zakat ul fitr is the money you pay to the poor before the Eid. So also they can celebrate the day of Eid.

Make your sadaqah bottle

To encourage friends and family to remind them of giving sadaqah, you can make a sadaqah bottle. Clean a used plastic bottle and paint sadaqah on it with nice letters. You can also copy a hadith about sadaqah on it. Make an opening in the bottle so people can put money in it. When the bottle is full, give the money to a charity project and make your New sadaqah bottle.

Narrated Anas(RA): The Prophet (SAW) said:"None of you will have faith till he likes for his brother what he likes for himself."

Talk about this hadith with others. What does it mean?

What does this have to do with the money in your wallet?

Eid ulFitr

The new moon is seen and Ramadan has ended. Muslims are happy they completed the month by fasting and they can celebrate the day of Eid.

You can use a checklist to see if you have thought about everything.

Checklist

	Is the Zakat ulfitr paid?
	To which masjid you go for the Eid prayer?
	What time does the Salatul Eid starts?
	Is the house tidy to invite guests? Did you invite guests?
	Ask your mum and dad: can I help you?
	Did you have a bath early in the morning?
	Are your Eid clothes ready?
	You know how the Eid prayer goes? You know what to say on your way to the masjid?

Eid party

If you know that a lot of children will come to your house on the day of Eid as well, you can think of some games to do.

You can also ask your mother and father to invite your friends on a time what suits them.

Discuss with your parents which games are suitable and what you can eat.

For this occasion you can also make an invitation card.

invitation for the party

day	time	address and telephonenumber

Arts

Collect all kinds of stones, coloured glass and make an ornament in clay. Reuse materials, it does not need to cost a lot of money.

Visit the sick and bring them self made presents

In advance you can ask who is ill at home or in hospital. Try to visit them and bring them some fruit, cookies or food from the party.

Cookies

Make cookie dough and let everyone make his own cookie. At the end of the party you can eat your self-made cookie or let them take home.

Make your Eid party preparation

Children
Who are you inviting for the party?

Invitations
Phone or write cards and tell place, time of party

Food What to buy and what to cook?
Drinks

Games
Prepare what you need to play the games.

Arts
Get the materials you want to use.

Schedule
Make a time planning
What first, next, last

Awards
Prepare the awards for your activities

Work together in a good way, give compliments and don't be angry about mistakes

Quiz

Make teams of two, three or four and let one of the adults ask questions about Ramadan.
The teams fill in the answers on a paper. At the end the group with the most right answers get a little prize. You can think of extra sweets or an award. You can make different awards, so everyone can go home with his or her award.
You can make a quiz the way you like it. Make sure everyone understands the game. Make of the game an exciting time, so everyone will enjoy.

Start with the easy questions to get everyone warmed up!

- To give the answer there are different options.
- Let them write down the answer.
- Let them choose the right answer from 4 answers you tell them.

Make it fun!

When you play the quiz outside and you have the space you can also make a run game. On the other side of the field is a bell. The one who runs first to the bell is allowed to give the answer first. If it is the wrong answer the others can give it a try.

You can also let the children ask for a category. They run to the bell and they can choose a question from a certain category.

Categories can be:

- Prophets
- Life of the prophet Muhammad (SAW)
- Knowledge of Arabic
- The sunah of the prophet Muhammad (SAW)
- Quran

Write the questions on cards, with the answer.Put the cards from the same category in an envelope and give them a number.
Then it is easier to find the question you need.
When the child has given the right answer, he or she can keep the card.

Start when everyone understands the rules

Quiz questions, just a start and you can make more or other questions. It depends on the age of the children as well.

Prophets

- Which prophet was 40 days in the belly of a whale?
- Which prophet could control the winds and speak with animals?
- Which prophet could make the dead alive?
- Which prophet built an ark?
- Which prophet had a stick what could turn into a snake?

Life of the prophet Muhammad(SAW)

- The prophet Muhammad (SAW) was also called El Ameen? What does it mean?
- At what age did the prophet Muhammad (SAW)start receiving the revelations?
- In which month did the revelations started?
- What was the name of the wife of the prophet Muhammad (SAW)when he starts receiving the messages from Allah (SWT)?
- Who was a companion of the prophet Muhammad (SAW)?

Knowledge of Arabic

- What does sunnah mean?
- What does saum mean?
- What is laylatulQadr?
- What does sadaqah mean?

The sunnah of the prophet Muhammad (SAW)

- What do we do before we pray?
- What is the best place to pray for men?
- What is the best place for women to pray?
- What do you say when you meet your Muslim brother or sister?
- What do we say when we start something?

Quran

- How many surahshas the Quran?
- What is the name of the first surah of the Quran?
- In which surah is explained about the event with the elephants?
- What means Al Furqan?
- What means Taqwah?
- Which surah is the longest surah of the Quran?

(creative artist award, wonderful reciter, thank you for being there award, choose what you like and prepare them in advance so you can fill in the right name and hand it out on the day) your friends will feel really happy and proud Insha Allah. If you want to have ready-made awards check the website www.aichatou.com)

What was very special to you this Ramadan and what did you learn? Ask your parents, brothers, sisters also to write something for you.

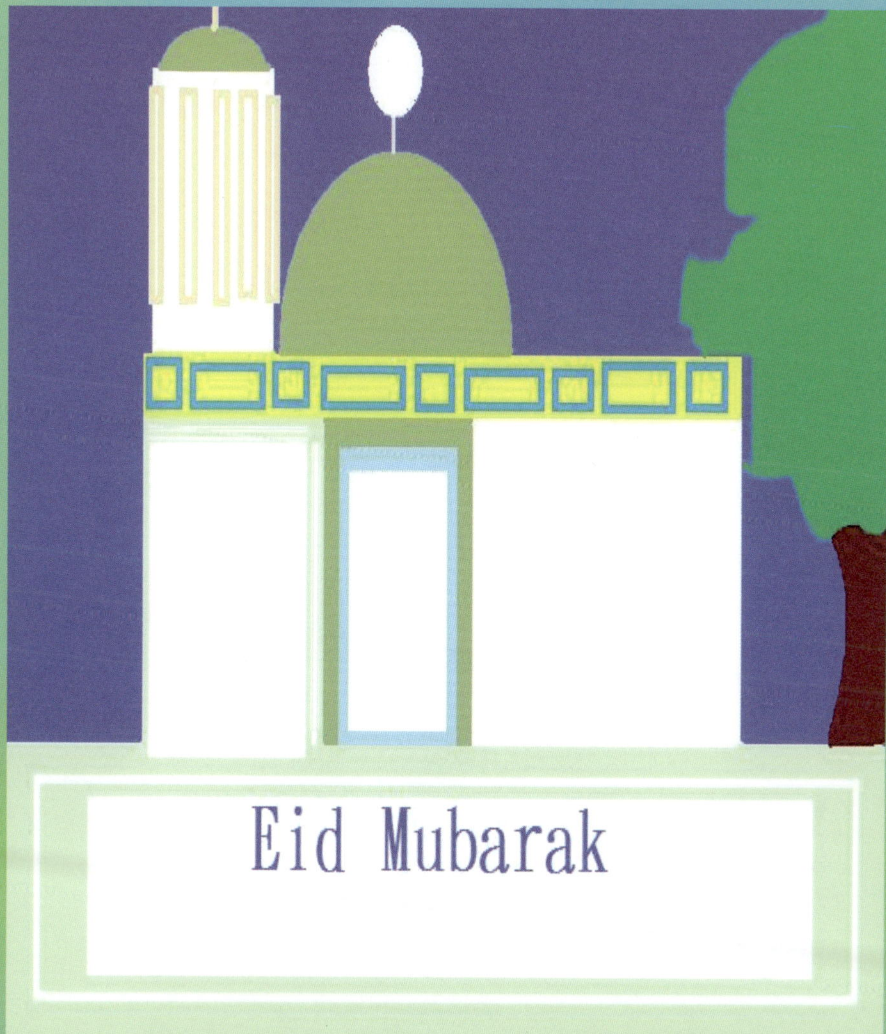

Mashallah you have completed this workbook! May knowledge help you and your family throughout the whole year Insha Allah.

Glossary

Ayah: Part of a surah

Hadith:Collected reports of the words and deeds of the prophet Muhammad (SAW)

Halal: Everything what Allah (SWT) approves to do, eat or use.

Haram:Everything Allah forbids us to do, eat or use.

Ibadah:Worshipping and loving Allah (SWT) by being obedient to Him. Loving the halal and hating and staying away from the haram.

Iftar:The evening meal when Muslims break their fast. It is done right after Magrib, sunset time.

I'tikaf:a period of retreat in a mosque for a certain number of days according to your own wish.
I'tikaf is very common in the last ten days of Ramadan.

LailatulQadr: The night of Power which you can find in the odd nights of the last ten days of Ramadan. In this night theProphet Muhammad (SAW) received the first revelation of the Quran.

Sadaqah:Voluntary charity you spend on the poor. It includes as well any act of giving like love, friendship, generosity

Salaat: The obligatory daily prayer of a Muslim. This prayer is one of the pillars of Islam.You pray at a prescribed time, in a prescribed manner and the prayer has prescribed conditions.

Sunnah: thehabits, customs and usual practise of the prophet Muhammad (SAW) and what he approved silently.

Suhoor: The meal consumed early in the morning before fasting starts.

Surah: a chapter of the Quran.

Time management: Controlling the way you spend your time and divide your time.

Waning moon: shrinking moon

Waxing moon: growing moon

Zakat: The obligatory payment of 2.5% of your wealth what you have to pay to the poor. It is one of the 5 pillars of Islam.

Ramadan fasting and striving for Jannah by Aichatou

More books and educational material at www.aichatou.com